HAMMER BLOWS AND OTHER WRITINGS

DAVID MANDESSI DIOP

DAVID MANDESSI DIOP

HAMMER BLOWS AND OTHER WRITINGS

TRANSLATED AND EDITED BY SIMON MPONDO AND FRANK JONES

Indiana University Press / Bloomington and London

CONTENTS

v

ACKNOWLEDGMENTS

For permission to reprint copyright material, the editors are indebted to Editions Présence Africaine, who, in consideration of the educational purpose of the book, were most liberal with their aid. H. G. Jones, the man for all seasons in the house, suggested the translation of the title, and also carried on long and laborious detective work toward unearthing bibliographical information.

Most of the biographical data were generously provided by the poet's friend, Bakary Traoré.

The translations were twice presented and discussed in Frank Jones' seminar in translation at the University of Washington. We were greatly helped by the comments offered in these classes.

SIMON MPONDO
Professor of English and
African Literature
Federal University of Cameroon

FRANK JONES
Professor of English and
Comparative Literature
University of Washington

TEXTUAL AND BIBLIOGRAPHICAL NOTE

The poems printed here under the subtitle "Coups de Pilon / Hammer Blows" constitute the entire contents of Diop's only published book, *Coups de Pilon* (Paris: Présence Africaine, 1956). Its title means, literally, *Pestle Blows,* alluding to the large pestles used to crush grain in African villages.

For the third line from the end of the dedicatory poem we have followed its first published text (*Présence Africaine,* No. 32/33), which has *la voix,* instead of *ta voix,* as in *Coups de Pilon,* so that the speaker, rather than asking his mother to listen to her own voice, is addressing the world at large.

Another translation of this poem was published in that issue of *Présence Africaine,* and English versions of seven other poems by Diop are to be found in *Modern Poetry from Africa,* edited by Gerald Moore and Ulli Beier (Penguin Books, 1963).

The poems in the present book were translated jointly by the editors. Diop's remarks on the Bandoeng conference, which first appeared in *Présence Africaine,* No. 3, were translated by Frank Jones. The essay on education in Guinea is taken from the English edition of *Présence Africaine,* No. 29. Simon Mpondo translated the other prose pieces, wrote the biographical note and the critical essay, and compiled the glossary. His essay is much revised and enlarged from the version published in *Présence Africaine,* No. 75.

COUPS DE PILON

HAMMER BLOWS

A MA MÉRE

Quand autour de moi surgissent les souvenirs
Souvenirs d'escales anxieuses au bord du gouffre
De mers glacées où se noient les moissons
Quand revivent en moi les jours à la dérive
Les jours en lambeaux à goût de narcotique
Où derrière les volets clos
Le mot se fait aristocrate pour enlacer le vide
Alors mère je pense à toi
A tes belles paupières brûlées par les années
A ton sourire sur mes nuits d'hôpital
Ton sourire qui disait les vieilles misères vaincues
O mère mienne et qui est celle de tous
Du nègre qu'on aveugla et qui revoit les fleurs
Ecoute ecoute la voix
Elle est ce cri traversé de violence
Elle est ce chant guidé seul par l'amour.

When memories rise around me
Memories of anxious halts on the edge of the abyss
Of icy seas where harvests drown
When days of drifting live in me again
Days in rags with a narcotic flavor
When behind closed shutters
The word turns aristocrat to embrace the void
Then mother I think of you
Your beautiful eyelids scorched by the years
Your smile on my hospital nights
Your smile that spoke old vanquished miseries
O mother mine and mother of all
Of the negro who was blinded and sees the flowers
    again
Listen listen to the voice
This is the cry shot through with violence
This is the song whose only guide is love.

LES VAUTOURS

En ce temps-là
A coups de gueule de civilisation
A coups d'eau bénite sur les fronts domestiqués
Les vautours construisaient à l'ombre de leurs serres
Le sanglant monument de l'ère tutélaire
En ce temps-là
Les rires agonisaient dans l'enfer métallique des routes
Et le rhythme monotone des Pater-Noster
Couvrait les hurlements des plantations à profit
O le souvenir acide des baisers arrachés
Les promesses mutilées au choc des mitrailleuses
Hommes étranges qui n'étiez pas des hommes
Vous saviez tous les livres vous ne saviez pas l'amour
Et les mains qui fécondent le ventre de la terre
Les racines de nos mains profondes comme la révolte
Malgré vos chants d'orgueil au milieu des charniers
Les villages désolés l'Afrique écartelée
L'espoir vivait en nous comme une citadelle
Et des mines du Souaziland à la sueur lourde
    des usines d'Europe
Le printemps prendra chair sous nos pas de clarté.

THE VULTURES

In that time
When civilization struck with insults
When holy water struck domesticated brows
The vultures built in the shadow of their claws
The bloody monument of the tutelary era
In that time
Laughter gasped its last in the metallic hell of roads
And the monotonous rhythm of Paternosters
Covered the groans on plantations run for profit
O sour memory of extorted kisses
Promises mutilated by machine-gun blasts
Strange men who were not men
You knew all the books you did not know love
Or the hands that fertilize the womb of the earth
The roots of our hands deep as revolt
Despite your hymns of pride among boneyards
Villages laid waste and Africa dismembered
Hope lived in us like a citadel
And from the mines of Swaziland to the heavy sweat of
        Europe's factories
Spring will put on flesh under our steps of light.

LA ROUTE VÉRITABLE

Frères dont on voudrait déchirer la jeunesse
Ne cherchez pas la vérité dans la grimace de leurs phrases
Dans leurs claques paternelles et les trahisons d'alcôve
Ne cherchez pas la beauté dans ce masque qui s'agite
Et sature de parfums la hideur de leurs plaies
Non plus l'amour dans ces cuisses dévoilées
Monnayant l'aventure dans les bars à prétexte
La vérité la beauté l'amour
C'est l'ouvrier brisant le calme meurtrier de leurs salons
C'est la femme qui passe sensuelle et grave
Le baiser qui franchit les frontières du calcul
Et les fleurs des fiancés et l'enfant dans les bras aimés
C'est tout ce qu'ils ont perdu frères
Et qu'ensemble nous déroulerons sur les chemins du monde.

Brothers whose youth they would like to tear asunder
Do not seek truth in the grimace of their phrases
In their patronizing claques and bedroom treasons
Do not seek beauty in the twitching mask
That soaks in scent the ugliness of their wounds
Or love in those unveiled thighs
Peddling adventure in delusive bars
Truth beauty love are
The worker smashing the deadly calm of their parlors
The woman passing by sensual and serious
The kiss that crosses the frontiers of reckoning
And flowers of engaged couples and the child in loved arms
Everything they have lost brothers
And that we together will unfold on the highways of the world.

LES HEURES

Il y a des heures pour rêver
Dans l'apaisement des nuits au creux du silence
Il y a des heures pour douter
Et le lourd voile des mots se déchire en sanglots
Il y a des heures pour souffrir
Le long des chemins de guerre dans le regard des mères
Il y a des heures pour aimer
Dans les cases de lumière où chante la chair unique
Il y a ce qui colore les jours à venir
Comme le soleil colore la chair des plantes
Et dans le délire des heures
Dans l'impatience des heures
Le germe toujours plus fécond
Des heures d'où naîtra l'équilibre.

There are hours for dreaming
In the calmness of nights in the hollow of silence
There are hours for doubting
And the heavy veil of words is torn in sobs
There are hours for suffering
Along the roads of war in the look of mothers
There are hours for loving
In the huts of light where the unique flesh sings
There is that which colors days to come
As the sun colors the flesh of plants
And in the delirium of hours
In the impatience of hours
The ever more fertile seed
Of hours from which equilibrium will be born.

L'AGONIE DES CHAÎNES

Dimbokro Poulo Condor
La ronde des hyènes autour des cimetières
La terre gorgée de sang les képis qui ricanent
Et sur les routes le grondement sinistre des charrettes
   de haine
Je pense au Vietnamien couché dans la rizière
Au forçat du Congo frère du lynché d'Atlanta
Je pense au cheminement macabre du silence
Quand passe l'aile d'acier sur les rires à peine nés
Dimbokro Poulo Condor
Ils croyaient aux chaines qui étranglent l'espoir
Au regard qu'on éteint sous l'éternelle sueur
Pourtant c'est le soleil qui jaillit de nos voix
Et des savanes aux jungles
Nos mains crispées dans l'étreinte du combat
Montrent à ceux qui pleurent des éclats d'avenir
Dimbokro Poulo Condor
Entendez-vous bruire la sève souterraine
C'est la chanson des morts
La chanson qui nous porte aux jardins de la vie.

THE AGONY OF CHAINS

Dimbokro Poulo Condor
The prowl of hyenas around graveyards
The earth gorged with blood the mocking helmets
And on the roads the sinister rattle of carts of hatred
I think of the Vietnamese crouched in the rice paddy
The Congo convict brother of the man they lynched
     in Atlanta
I think of the deathly spread of silence
When the steel wing passes over laughter freshly born
Dimbokro Poulo Condor
They believed in chains that strangle hope
In the look extinguished under everlasting sweat
And yet the sun spurts from our voices
And from savannas to jungles
Our fists clenched in the grip of battle
Show flashes of future to those who weep
Dimbokro Poulo Condor
Do you hear the sap rumble underground
It is the song of the dead
The song that carries us to the gardens of life.

A UNE DANSEUSE NOIRE

Négresse ma chaude rumeur d'Afrique
Ma terre d'énigme et mon fruit de raison
Tu es danse par la joie nue de ton sourire
Par l'offrande de tes seins et tes secrets pouvoirs
Tu es danse par les légendes d'or des nuits nuptiales
Par les temps nouveaux et les rythmes séculaires
Négresse triomphe multiplié de rêves et d'étoiles
Maîtresse docile à l'étreinte des koras
Tu es danse par le vertige
Par la magie des reins recommençant le monde
Tu es danse
Et les mythes autour de moi brûlent
Autour de moi les perruques du savoir
En grands feux de joie dans le ciel de tes pas
Tu es danse
Et brûlent les faux dieux sous ta flamme verticale
Tu es le visage de l'initié
Sacrifiant la folie auprès l'arbre-gardien
Tu es l'idée du Tout et la voix de l'Ancien.
Lancée grave à l'assaut des chimères
Tu es le Verbe qui explose
En gerbes miraculeuses sur les côtes de l'oubli.

Negress my hot uproar of Africa
My land of riddle and my fruit of reason
You are dance by the naked joy of your smile
By the offering of your breasts and your secret powers
You are dance by golden legends of bridal nights
By new times and ancestral rhythms
Negress multiple triumph of dreams and stars
Mistress obedient to the embrace of Koras
You are dance by dizziness
By the magic of loins beginning the world anew
You are dance
And around me the myths burn
Around me the wigs of learning
In great fires of joy in the sky of your steps
You are dance
And the false gods burn beneath your vertical flame
You are the face of the initiate
Sacrificing madness beside the guardian tree
You are the idea of the All and the voice of the Ancient.
Gravely launched to attack chimeras
You are the Word that explodes
In miraculous spray on the shores of oblivion.

ENSEMBLE

A Jwyé
Ensemble t'en souviens-tu nous faisions la parade
Sur les tombes alignées
Nous étions le geste machinal
Traduisant en profits l'espérance des hommes
Et nos bouches collées aux mamelles flétries
Attendaient une aumône goutte à goutte tirée
Tout était sali
Il n'y avait plus de temps sur les troupeaux domptés
Plus rien qu'un trou immense
Et les longues dents dures des nuits sans amour
Est-ce toi qui le premier découvris les couleurs
Qu'importe nous sommes là ensemble comme avant
Nos maux sont devenus les armes du réel
Et debout enfin progressant contre l'ombre
Nous regardons la terre mûrir à la raison.

VAGUES

Les vagues furieuses de la liberté
Claquent claquent sur la Bête affolée
De l'esclave d'hier un combattant est né
Et le docker de Suez et le coolie d'Hanoi
Tous ceux qu'on intoxiqua de fatalité
Lancent leur chant immense au milieu des vagues
Les vagues furieuses de la liberté
Qui claquent claquent sur la Bête affolée.

14

for Jwyé
Together you remember we paraded
Along the rows of tombs
We were the mechanical gesture
Translating man's hopes into profits
And our mouths glued to blighted nipples
Awaited alms squeezed drop by drop
Everything was soiled
No time was left on the subdued herds
Nothing but an enormous hole
And long hard teeth of loveless nights
Were you the first to discover colors
Never mind we are here together as before
Our woes have become the weapons of the real
And standing up at last advancing against the dark
We watch the earth ripen to reason.

WAVES

The raging waves of freedom
Slap slap against the maddened Beast
Of yesterday's slave a fighter is born
And the Suez docker and the Hanoi coolie
All who were drugged with fatality
Launch their immense song amid the waves
The raging waves of freedom
That slap slap against the maddened Beast.

AUX MYSTIFICATEURS

Monstres cyniques en cigare
Véhiculés d'orgies en vols
Et baladant l'égalité dans une cage de fer
Vous prêchiez la tristesse enchaînée à la peur
Le chant mélancolique et le renoncement
Et vos mantes démentes
Précipitant la mort sur chaque été naissant
Inventaient le cauchemar des pas cadencés dans
       les cirques à nègres
Aujourd'hui vos cités interdites
S'ouvrent en pleurs tardifs en serments solennels
Et vos paroles de sucre inépuisablement rampent
Entre les ruines accumulées
C'est l'heure où vos penseurs soudain pris de douleurs
Accouchent en chœur de l'unité
Et convertissent l'éclair en clinquant monotone
Mais qui cédera à l'invisible torpeur
Aux pièges tissés autour du berceau vermoulu
Qui cédera aux trompettes du baptême
Alors qu'éclatent les cordes au vent dur
Et que meurent les mascarades mordues de roc en roc
Il suffit du frisson du maïs
Du cri l'arachide martelant la faim nègre
Pour diriger nos pas vers la droite lumière
Et à vos nuits d'alcool à propagande
A vos nuits écrasées de saluts automatiques
A vos nuits de pieux silence et de sermons sans fin
Nous opposons l'hymne aux muscles bandés
Qui salue l'étincelant départ
L'hymne insolite de l'Afrique en haillons
Déchirant les ténèbres établis pour mille ans.

Cynical monsters flashing cigars
Riding on flights of orgies
And parading equality in an iron cage
You preached sadness chained to fear
Melancholy song and renunciation
And your mad mantises
Making death swoop on every summer born
Invented the nightmare of marching steps in negro circuses
Today your forbidden cities
Open in belated tears in solemn oaths
And your sugary words creep tirelessly
Among heaps of ruins
This is the hour when your thinkers seized with sudden cramps
Give birth to unity in chorus
And convert the lightning into monotonous tinfoil
Which however will yield to invisible torpor
And traps woven around the worm-eaten cradle
Which will yield to the trumpets of baptism
When the ropes split in the harsh wind
And the bitten masquerades die from rock to rock
It needs but a rustle of corn
A cry of the groundnut hammering negro hunger
To guide our steps toward straight light
And against your nights of alcoholic propaganda
Your nights crushed by automatic greetings
Your nights of pious silence and endless sermons
We set the taut-muscled hymn
That greets the sparkling departure
The unfamiliar hymn of tattered Africa
Cracking the settled gloom of a thousand years.

LE RENÉGAT

Mon frère aux dents qui brillent sous le
    compliment hypocrite
Mon frère aux lunettes d'or
Sur tes yeux rendus bleus par la parole du Maître
Mon pauvre frère au smoking à revers de soie
Piaillant et susurrant et plastronnant dans les salons de la
    condescendance
Tu nous fais pitié
Le soleil de ton pays n'est plus qu'une ombre
Sur ton front serein de civilisé
Et la case de ta grand'mère
Fait rougir un visage blanchi par les années d'humiliation
    et de Mea Culpa
Mais lorsque repu de mots sonores et vides
Comme la caisse qui surmonte tes épaules
Tu fouleras la terre amère et rouge d'Afrique
Ces mots angoissés rythmeront alors ta marche inquiète
Je me sens seul si seul ici!

My brother with teeth that flash to
    hypocritical compliments
My brother with gold-rimmed glasses
Over eyes turned blue by the Master's word
My poor brother with silk-lined dinner jacket
Squeaking and droning and strutting in the parlors of
    condescension
We find you pitiable
Your country's sun is nothing but a shadow
On your serenely civilized brow
And your grandmother's hut
Brings blushes to a face whitened by years of humiliation
    and Mea Culpa
But when stuffed with empty echoing words
Like the box that surmounts your shoulders
You tread the bitter red earth of Africa
Then these anguished words will mark your troubled steps
I feel alone here so alone!

ÉCOUTEZ CAMARADES . . .

Ecoutez camarades des siècles d'incendie
L'ardente clameur nègre d'Afrique aux Amériques
Ils ont tué Mamba
Comme là-bas les sept de Martinsville
Comme le Malgache là-bas dans le crépitement blème des prisons
Il y avait dans son regard camarades
La chaude fidélité d'un cœur sans angoisse
Et son sourire par delà les souffrances
Par delà les blessures sur son corps labouré
Gardait les claires couleurs d'un bouquet d'espérance
C'est vrai qu'ils l'ont tué Mamba aux cheveux blancs
Qui dix fois nous versa le lait et la lumière
Je sens sa bouche sur mes rèves
Et le frémissement paisible de sa poitrine
Et ma mémoire a mal
Comme la plante arrachée hors du sein maternel
Mais non
Voici qu'éclate plus haut que ma douleur
Plus pur que le matin où s'éveilla le fauve
Le cri de cent peuples écrasant les tanières
Et mon sang d'années d'exil
Le sang qu'ils crurent tarir dans le cercueil des mots
Retrouve la ferveur qui transperce les brumes
Ecoutez camarades des siècles d'incendie
L'ardente clameur nègre d'Afrique aux Amériques
C'est le signe de l'aurore
Le signe fraternel qui viendra nourrir le rêve des hommes.

Listen comrades of incendiary centuries
To the flaming black outcry from Africa to the Americas
They have killed Mamba
As they did the seven at Martinsville
As they did the Malagasy in the livid crackle of prisons
In his look comrades there was
The warm fidelity of an untormented heart
And beyond the pain
Beyond the wounds on his flailed body
His smile kept the bright colors of a bouquet of hope
It's true they've killed him white-haired Mamba
Who ten times poured us milk and light
On my dreams I feel his mouth
And the calm throb of his breast
And my memory hurts
Like the plant torn from the maternal womb
But no
Now higher than my grief
Purer than the morning when the wild beast woke
Bursts the cry of a hundred peoples smashing dens
And the blood of my years of exile
Blood they thought was running dry in the coffin of words
Regains the fervor that pierces fogs
Listen comrades of incendiary centuries
To the flaming black outcry from Africa to the Americas
It is the sign of dawn
The fraternal sign that will come and feed the dreams of men.

AUPRÈS DE TOI

Auprès de toi j'ai retrouvé mon nom
Mon nom longtemps caché sous le sel des distances
J'ai retrouvé les yeux que ne voilent plus les fièvres
Et ton rire comme la flamme trouant l'ombre
M'a redonné l'Afrique au delà des neiges d'hier
Dix ans mon amour
Et les matins d'illusions et les débris d'idées
Et les sommeils peuplés d'alcool
Dix ans et le souffle du monde m'a versé sa souffrance
Cette souffrance qui charge le présent du goût des lendemains
Et fait de l'amour un fleuve sans mesure
Auprès de toi j'ai retrouvé la mémoire de mon sang
Et les colliers de rires autour des jours
Les jours qui étincellent de joies renouvelées.

Close to you I have regained my name
My name long hidden beneath the salt of distances
I have regained eyes no longer veiled by fevers
And your laugh like a flame making holes in the dark
Has given Africa back to me beyond the snows of yesterday
Ten years my love
And mornings of illusion and wreckage of ideas
And sleep peopled with alcohol
Ten years and the breath of the world has poured its
    pain upon me
Pain that loads the present with the flavor of tomorrows
And makes of love an immeasurable river
Close to you I have regained the memory of my blood
And necklaces of laughter around the days
Days that sparkle with joys renewed.

AFRIQUE

à ma Mère
Afrique mon Afrique
Afrique des fiers guerriers dans les savanes ancestrales
Afrique que chante ma grand'Mère
Au bord de son fleuve lointain
Je ne t'ai jamais connue
Mais mon regard est plein de ton sang
Ton beau sang noir à travers les champs répandu
Le sang de ta sueur
La sueur de ton travail
Le travail de l'esclavage
L'esclavage de tes enfants
Afrique dis-moi Afrique
Est-ce donc toi-ce dos qui se courbe
Et se couche sous le poids de l'humilité
Ce dos tremblant à zébrures rouges
Qui dit oui au fouet sur les routes de midi
Alors gravement une voix me répondit
Fils impétueux cet arbre robuste et jeune
Cet arbre là-bas
Splendidement seul au milieu de fleurs blanches et fanées
C'est l'Afrique ton Afrique qui repousse
Qui repousse patiemment obstinément
Et dont les fruits ont peu à peu
L'amère saveur de la liberté.

to my Mother
Africa my Africa
Africa of proud warriors in ancestral savannas
Africa of which my grandmother sings
Beside her faraway river
I never knew you
But my gaze is full of your blood
Your beautiful black blood spilt in the fields
The blood of your sweat
The sweat of your toil
The toil of slavery
The slavery of your children
Africa tell me Africa
Can this be you the back that bends
And lies flat beneath the weight of humility
This trembling red-striped back
Saying yes to the whip along the roads of noon
Then a voice answered me gravely
Impetuous son the young and hardy tree
You see there
Splendidly alone among white and faded flowers
Is Africa your Africa growing again
Growing again patiently stubbornly
With fruits that take on little by little
The bitter taste of freedom.

A UN ENFANT NOIR

Quinze ans
Et la vie comme une promesse un royaume entrevu

Dans le pays où les maisons touchent le ciel
Mais où le cœur n'est pas touché
Dans le pays où l'on pose la main sur la Bible
Mais où la Bible n'est pas ouverte
La vie à quinze ans apaise la faim des fleuves
La vie des peaux d'enfer des nom-de-Dieu de nègres
L'enfant noir un soir d'août perpétra le crime
Il osa l'infâme se servir des ses yeux
Et son regard rêva sur une bouche sur des seins sur un
    corps de Blanche
Ce corps enfant noir que seul aux sex-parties
Le Blanc peut saccager au rythme de tes blues
(Le nègre quelquefois sous des murs anonymes)
Le crime ne paie pas te l'avait-on assez dit
Et pour que justice soit faite ils furent deux
Juste deux sur le plateau de la balance
Deux hommes sur tes quinze ans et le royaume entrevu
Ils pensèrent à l'aveugle fou qui voyait
Aux femmes éclaboussées
Au règne qui trébuchait
Et ta tête vola sous les rires hystériques.

Dans les villas climatisées
Autour des boissons fraîches
La bonne conscience savoure son repos.

TO A BLACK CHILD

Fifteen years
And life like a promise a glimpsed kingdom

In the land where houses touch the sky
But the heart is not touched
In the land where hands are laid on the Bible
But the Bible is not opened
Life at fifteen slakes the hunger of rivers
The life of the hellskins the goddam niggers
On an August evening the black child committed the crime
He infamously dared to use his eyes
And his look dreamed of a mouth of breasts of a White
      woman's body
The body black child which only a White
May ransack at sex parties to the beat of your blues
(The negro sometimes under nameless walls)
Crime doesn't pay they had told you often enough
And that justice might be done there were two of them
Exactly two on the pan of the scales
Two men on your fifteen years and the glimpsed kingdom
They thought of the mad blind man who saw
Of their women besmirched
Of their tottering rule
And your head flew off to hysterical laughter.

In air-conditioned mansions
Around cool drinks
An easy conscience relishes its rest.

CERTITUDE

à Alioune Diop
A ceux qui s'engraissent de meurtres
Et mesurent en cadavres les étapes de leur règne
Je dis que les jours et les hommes
Que le soleil et les étoiles
Dessinent le rythme fraternel des peuples
Je dis que le cœur et la tête
Se rejoignent dans la ligne droite du combat
Et qu'il n'est pas de jour
Où quelque part ne naisse l'été
Je dis que les tempêtes viriles
Ecraseront les marchands de patience
Et que les saisons sur les corps accordés
Verront se reformer les gestes du bonheur.

to Alioune Diop
To those who grow fat on murders
And measure the stages of their reign in corpses
I say that days and men
Sun and stars
Shape the fraternal rhythm of the peoples
I say that heart and head
Meet in the straight line of battle
And that there is no day
When somewhere summer is not born
I say that storms of manliness
Will crush the hawkers of patience
And that on bodies in accord the seasons
Will see the gestures of happiness take new form.

RAMA KAM

Chant pour une négresse
Me plaît ton regard de fauve
Et ta bouche à la saveur de mangue
    Rama Kam
Ton corps est le piment noir
Qui fait chanter le désir
    Rama Kam
Quand tu passes
La plus belle est jalouse
Du rythme chaleureux de ta hanche
    Rama Kam
Quand tu danses
Le tam-tam Rama-Kam
Le tam-tam tendu comme un sexe de victoire
Halète sous les doigts bondissants du griot
Et quand tu aimes
Quand tu aimes Rama Kam
C'est la tornade qui tremble
Dans ta chair de nuit d'éclairs
Et me laisse plein du souffle de toi
    O Rama Kam!

song for a negress
I like your wild beast look
And your mouth that tastes of mango
　　Rama Kam
Your body is black spice
That makes desire sing
　　Rama Kam
When you pass
The loveliest girl envies
The warm rhythm of your hips
　　Rama Kam
When you dance
The tomtom Rama Kam
The tomtom stretched like a victorious sex
Gasps under the drummer's leaping fingers
And when you love
When you love Rama Kam
A tornado quivers
In the lightning night of your flesh
And leaves me full of the breath of you
　　O Rama Kam!

NÈGRE CLOCHARD

à Aimé Césaire
Toi qui marchais comme un vieux rêve brisé
Un rêve foudroyé sous les lames du mistral
Par quels chemins de sel
Par quels détours de boue de souffrance acceptée
Par quelles caravelles plantant d'îles en îles
Les drapeaux de sang nègre arrachés de Guinée
As-tu conduit ta défroque d'épines
Jusqu'au cimetière étrange où tu lisais le ciel
Je vois dans tes yeux les haltes courbées de désespoir
Et l'aube recommençant le coton et les mines
Je vois Soundiata l'oublié
Et Chaka l'indomptable
Enfouis au fond des mers avec les contes de soie et de feu
Je vois tout cela
Des musiques martiales claironnant l'appel au meurtre
Et des ventres qui s'ouvrent dans des paysages de neige
Pour rassurer la peur tapie au creux des villes
O mon vieux nègre moissonneur de terres inconnues
Terres odorantes où chacun pouvait vivre
Qu'ont-ils fait de l'aurore qui s'ouvrait sur ton front
De tes pierres lumineuses et de tes sabres d'or
Te voici nu dans ta prison fangeuse
Volcan éteint offert aux rires des autres
A la richesse des autres
A la faim hideuse des autres
Ils t'appelaient Blanchette c'était si pittoresque
Et ils secouaient leurs grandes gueules à principes
Heureux du joli mot pas méchants pour un sou
Mais moi moi qu'ai-je fait dans ton matin de
     vent et de larmes
Dans ce matin noyé d'écume
Où pourrissaient les couronnes sacrées

to Aimé Césaire
You who walked like an old broken dream
A dream blasted by the stabbing mistral
On what salt roads
What muddy byways of accepted pain
What caravels planting from isle to isle
The flags of negro blood that were torn from Guinea
Did you take the thorns of your tattered clothes
To the strange graveyard where you read the sky
I see in your eyes the crouching stops of despair
And the dawn that starts the cotton and the mines again
I see forgotten Sundiata
And unconquerable Chaka
Sunk in the ocean floor with tales of silk and fire
I see it all
Martial music trumpeting calls to murder
And bellies opening in snowy landscapes
To calm the fear that huddles in city depths
O my old negro reaper of unknown lands
Fragrant lands where anyone could live
What have they done to the dawn that was opening
    on your brow
To your gleaming stones and your golden sabres
Here you are naked in your filthy jail
Extinct volcano exposed to the laughter of others
The wealth of others
The hideous hunger of others
They called you Snow White how quaint that was
And they wagged their big principled snouts
Delighted by the neat phrase not mean at all
But I I what did I do on your windy tearful morning
The morning drowned in foam
When the sacred crowns decayed

Qu'ai-je fait sinon supporter assis sur mes nuages
Les agonies nocturnes
Les blessures immuables
Les guenilles pétrifiées dans les camps d'épouvante
Le sable était de sang
Et je voyais le jour pareil aux autres jours
Et je chantais Yéba
Yéba à pleine folie les zoos en délire
O plantes enterrées
O semences perdues
Pardonne nègre mon guide
Pardonne mon cœur étroit
Les victoires retardées l'armure abandonnée
Patience le Carnaval est mort
J'aiguise l'ouragan pour les sillons futurs
Pour toi nous referons Ghâna et Tombouctou
Et les guitares peuplées de galops frénétiques
A grands coups de pilons sonores
De pilons
Eclatant
De case en case
Dans l'azur pressenti.

What did I do but bear seated on my clouds
Nocturnal agonies
Immovable wounds
Petrified rags in camps of terror
The sand was bloody
And I saw that day just like other days
And I sang Yeba
Yeba in utter madness zoos in delirium
O buried plants
O lost seeds
Negro my guide forgive
Forgive my narrow heart
Victories postponed abandoned armor
Patience the Carnival is dead
I whet the hurricane for future furrows
For you we will remake Ghana and Timbuktu
And guitars peopled with frantic gallops
To the sound of mighty pestle blows
Pestles
Bursting
From hut to hut
In the foreknown azure.

EARLIER POEMS

CELUI QUI A TOUT PERDU

Le soleil brillait dans ma case
Et mes femmes étaient belles et souples
Comme les palmiers sous la brise des soirs.
Mes enfants glissaient sur le grand fleuve
Aux profondeurs de mort
Et mes pirogues luttaient avec les crocodiles.
La lune, maternelle, accompagnait nos danses
Le rythme frénétique et lourd du tam-tam,
Tam-tam de la joie, tam-tam de l'insouciance
    Au milieu des feux de liberté.

Puis un jour, le Silence . . .
Les rayons du soleil semblèrent s'éteindre
Dans ma case vide de sens.
Mes femmes écrasèrent leurs bouches rougies
Sur les lèvres minces et dures des conquérants aux yeux d'acier
Et mes enfants quittèrent leur nudité paisible
Pour l'uniforme de fer et de sang.
Votre voix s'est éteinte aussi
Les fers de l'esclavage ont déchiré mon cœur
Tams-tams de mes nuits, tam-tams de mes pères.

The sun used to laugh in my hut
And my women were lovely and lissome
Like palms in the evening breeze.
My children would glide over the mighty river
Of deadly depths
And my canoes would battle with crocodiles.
The motherly moon accompanied our dances
The heavy frantic rhythm of the tomtom,
Tomtom of joy, tomtom of carefree life
    Amid the fires of liberty.

Then one day, Silence . . .
It seemed the rays of the sun went out
In my hut empty of meaning.
My women crushed their painted mouths
On the thin hard lips of steel-eyed conquerors
And my children left their peaceful nakedness
For the uniform of iron and blood.
Your voice went out too
The irons of slavery tore my heart to pieces
Tomtoms of my nights, tomtoms of my fathers.

LE TEMPS DU MARTYRE

à mon cher beau-frère, affectueusement
Le Blanc a tué mon père
Mon père était fier
Le Blanc a violé ma mère
Ma mère était belle
Le Blanc a courbé mon frère sous le soleil des routes
Mon frère était fort
Le Blanc a tourné vers moi
Ses mains rouges de sang
    Noir
Et de sa voix de Maître:
"Hé boy, un berger, une serviette, de l'eau!"

to my dear brother-in-law, with affection
The White killed my father
My father was proud
The White raped my mother
My mother was beautiful
The White bent my brother under the sun of the roads
My brother was strong
The White turned toward me
His hands red with black blood
And said in his Master's voice:
"Boy! An easy-chair, a towel, water!"

SOUFFRE, PAUVRE NÈGRE

Souffre, pauvre Nègre! . . .
Le fouet siffle
Siffle sur ton dos de sueur et de sang
Souffre, pauvre Nègre!
Le jour est long
Si long à porter l'ivoire blanc du Blanc ton Maître
Souffre, pauvre Nègre!
Tes enfants ont faim
Faim et ta case est vide
Vide de ta femme qui dort
Qui dort sur la couche seigneuriale.
Souffre, pauvre Nègre!
Nègre noir comme la Misère!

Suffer, poor Negro!
The whip whistles
Whistles on your back of sweat and blood
Suffer, poor Negro!
The day is long
So long for carrying the white ivory of the White your Master
Suffer, poor Negro!
Your children are hungry
Hungry and your hut is bare
Bare of your wife who is sleeping
Is sleeping on the seignorial couch.
Suffer, poor Negro!
Negro black as Misery!

UN BLANC M'A DIT . . .

Tu n'es qu'un nègre!
Un nègre!
Un sale nègre!
Ton cœur est une éponge qui boit
Qui boit avec frénésie le liquide empoisonné du Vice
Et ta couleur emprisonne ton sang
Dans l'éternité de l'esclavage.
Le fer rouge de la justice t'a marqué
Marqué dans ta chair de luxure.
Ta route a les contours tortueux de l'humiliation
Et ton avenir, monstre, damné, c'est ton présent de honte.
Donne-moi ce dos qui ruisselle
Et ruisselle de la sueur fétide de tes fautes.
Donne-moi tes mains calleuses et lourdes
Ces mains de rachat sans espoir.
Le travail n'attend pas!
Et que tombe ma pitié
Devant l'horreur de ton spectacle.

You're only a nigger!
A nigger!
A dirty nigger!
Your heart is a sponge that drinks
Frantically drinks the poisoned liquid of Vice
And your color imprisons your blood
In an eternity of slavery.
The red iron of justice has branded you
Branded your lecherous flesh.
You walk the twists and turns of humiliation
And your future, damned monster, is your shameful present.
Give me the back that streams
And streams with the rank sweat of your offenses.
Give me your heavy calloused hands
Those hands of hopeless atonement.
Work won't wait!
And may my pity drop
At the horror of your sight.

DÉFI À LA FORCE

Toi qui plies toi qui pleures
Toi qui meurs un jour comme ça sans savoir pourquoi
Toi qui luttes qui veilles pour le repos de l'Autre
Toi qui ne regardes plus avec le rire dans les yeux
Toi mon frère au visage de peur et d'angoisse
    Relève-toi et crie: NON!

You who bend you who weep
You who die one day just like that not knowing why
You who struggle and stay awake for the Other's rest
You with no more laughter in your look
You my brother with face of fear and anguish
    Rise and shout: NO!

PROSE

ON THE CONFERENCE AT BANDOENG

One of the most remarkable facts of the postwar period is, incontestably, the awakening of the so-called colored peoples.

Before the astonished gaze of Europe millions of human beings who until this epoch had undergone foreign domination and suffered the worst extortions, and had been inculcated with principles that were only a crude cover for sordid appetites, have discovered their strength and taken charge of their destiny. Playing innocent, the abusive "tutors" began talking of ingratitude and Communism, and hastened to reinforce the *cordon sanitaire* around whatever could still be saved. In spite of all, they had one hope left. As in the golden age of colonialism, could they not resume in recently liberated countries the good old policy of division? Perhaps there was a card to be played by persons interposed among the racial, religious, or political antagonists? The answer was Bandoeng.

It burst like a thunderclap in the tranquil offices of the imperialist brain trust.

The idea of a conference to bring together representatives of the independent powers of Asia and Africa had been put forward in April 1954, at Colombo, by the prime ministers of India, Ceylon, Indonesia, Burma, and Pakistan. A year later Indonesia welcomed to Bandoeng delegations from twenty-five countries which represented one billion four hundred million people, or more than one-half of humanity.

Some journalist or other might well wax ironic about this figure, and pretend to see in the conference something like "the great assizes of the inferiority complex." Facts remain facts, and they are not on his side.

For the first time in history, men of diverse races and tendencies, but united in hatred of colonialism and love of peace, proclaimed their will to fight tyranny everywhere and to defend their independence against all foreign interference.

Let impenitent colonialists make no mistake. The results of the

Bandoeng conference have a bearing far wider than they usually think.

They blazingly illustrate the fact that a new era is dawning for dependent countries and that from now on their fight for better living conditions will have the support of the young Afro-Asian nations. They, having known the abuses of colonization, will understand all the better the aspirations of those who are still enslaved.

The "intelligent" reactionaries grasped this so clearly that before and during the conference, using as intermediaries governments bound to them by economic ties, they tried to poison relations between the Communists and those who have come to be called neutralists. Their distractive maneuvers were swiftly laid bare by Nehru's clear-sightedness and the calm of those representing the people's China.

Incontestably, the conference at Bandoeng will be recorded in history as one of the decisive stages leading to the final triumph of peace.

ABOUT THE EDUCATIONAL REFORM
IN GUINEA

In an article devoted to the First Congress of Negro Writers and Artists, Alioune Diop wrote: "Our national cultures, like European culture, desire that, for the salvation of man, the dominated races and peoples should free themselves politically."[1]

It is, in fact, difficult to maintain that a regime based on economic exploitation and historical falsification (in this instance, the colonial regime) could encourage the flourishing of Negro cultures and give them dimensions adequate to the modern world. The reasons for this are diverse but primarily political. If an alien authority is to exercise itself with maximum effectiveness over the subject people, if the new order is to guarantee that the booty will be raked in, nothing must subsist to give that people a national consciousness. This is where the "theorists" of colonization come in, whose task is to turn Africa into "folklore," to replace its deep-seated values by picturesque and vaguely frightening representations, capable of interesting, at most, a handful of specialists.

"But you are behind the times," the "liberal" European will say, flanked by his Negro-alibi. "You are trying to scuttle a regime which is already obsolete everywhere. . . . The question today is to contribute to the creation of a new Eurafrican humanism." Obsolete? Hardly! . . . In Guinea where an unconstrained effort is being made toward total decolonization, yes. But elsewhere? In places where the Entente reigns, for example? In truth it is more a question of drowning the problem of national independence in so-called equalitarian and fraternal groupings, in which the "protector" will in fact continue to impose his nationalism and his culture on the "protected." It is therefore sheer hypocrisy to speak of the symbiosis of civilizations, and the reciprocal benefits to be found in a community whose universities do not even know the names of our great thinkers and pass over in silence the history of our empires. The only people who can accommodate themselves to it are the partisans of a cultural cosmopolitanism rigged out in exotic finery.

No need to dwell on this. *Présence Africaine* has sufficiently denounced this caricature of cooperation to make it unnecessary to revert to it. Our object is different.

It is to show, through the example of Guinea, that only full political sovereignty can, by liberating initiative, hasten the general evolution of Africa.

The fact is there, blindingly.

If, today, the Republic of Guinea can "go back to the cultural and moral sources of Africa, reintegrate her own consciousness, reconvert herself in her thoughts and acts, to the values, conditions and interests of Africa,"[2] it is because no external pressure, no high official tied to the colonial system, has the means to stop her.

In taking hold of her independence a year ago, Guinea ceased to be a thing tossed about under the paternalistic or brutal rod of the colonizer. From now on she is harnessed to the establishment of new structures and has finally undertaken to liquidate the inferiority complex created by a basically false education.

This education rested upon a sort of Manichaeism, both ingenuous and dangerous. On the one side, the West, with France at its head, steeped in art, culture, and lofty moral traditions; on the other side, an Africa withdrawn into its "asylum of barbarism," a prey to intestine struggles, saved by the coming of European peace. To convince oneself that there is no trace of exaggeration in these lines, it is enough to refer to any history book for the use of young Africans.

It was this too convenient interpretation of the history of the world that the Republic of Guinea attacked in setting up, in the very first months of independence, a Commission on Educational Reform.

After an exhaustive critical survey of the conception and orientation of colonial education, the leaders made every effort to give the school curriculum a content which would allow the African to rehabilitate himself in his own eyes and look at the world at last, not through the egocentric judgments of the colonizer, but on the basis of objective realities.

In future, in the schools of Guinea, the great events of history will no longer be the monopoly of the West. The West will cease to be the center of the world and Asia will be given a privileged place. The great revolutions of the twentieth century, Soviet and Chinese, prudently skated over in the old programs, will receive the full attention which they deserve, and the civilizations of Negro Africa, her political, social, and cultural achievements, will be studied in priority. In addition, and this is a fact of capital importance, the teaching of African languages will be made compulsory.

In literature, there has been an identical overthrow in the scale of values. This was all the more necessary, since the method previously used was to overload the curriculum with third-rate authors who did not even have the merit of representing the progressive current of European thought and with all haste to cram the young African with a mountain of texts alien to his feelings and to the needs of our time.

In breaking with the colonial "order" the Guinean nation has, at one blow, eliminated the danger from this kind of literature, which, in the words of a French critic, could not be anything more than "a series of anecdotes in the schoolroom, and in real life, the futile mourner of dead metaphysics." Freed from the lumber of formal cleverness and slyly sustained subtleties, literature is at last playing its full part, which is first and foremost that of creating and contributing to human progress. Thus, a large place is given to the Encyclopædists, to social romanticism, to the poets and novelists of every nationality who, in their works, have fought against injustice and borne witness in favor of human dignity. The accent is also placed on Negro authors, writing in the European languages, who have inspired the anti-imperialist struggle and sustained in the minds of young students the sense of personal responsibility and the taste for free inquiry.

There is therefore a real revolution, which, furthermore, extends to the scientific disciplines, and which, in conjunction with the planning of the Guinean economy, will give birth to a new type of African, bound to his cultural patrimony and open to the most fertile contributions from outside.

The objection will be raised that independence cannot magnificently solve all problems, that we must be on our guard against wide-mouthed optimism and the temptations of isolation. We would answer that it was colonialism which made Africa a closed preserve and isolated Africa from her natural surroundings and from the rest of the world. The independence of Guinea will certainly not create geniuses and masterpieces in some automatic fashion, but it has created the conditions for the free development of thought. It allows a candidate for the baccalaureate or the General Certificate of Education of today to uphold in a thesis without fear of rejection all the ideas which have so far been regarded as subversive. If one takes the trouble to look at the misdeeds of a self-censorship which, in the countries which are still dominated, shatters more surely than any law the creative impulse of the individual, one cannot deny the inestimable gain constituted by the conquest of political power.

We say again: nothing in the spirit or the letter of the reform betrays any wish to create a Guinea under glass, proudly rejecting outside help and practicing a sort of cultural narcissism. Far from it. The authors of the reform desired, by a twofold approach, to stimulate national energies by going back to African realities, and, on that basis, to establish with other nations relations which exclude all spirit of domination.

In this way the chasm will be bridged between the education which the young African received and the life which he was called upon to lead among his people. Turning their backs on the individualistic conceptions and intellectual anarchy proper to colonial education, Guinean students will henceforth be oriented toward a new road, where all the elements of national culture will become instruments of progress in the service of the people.

They will no longer be creatures without roots seeking a palliative for their solitude in chimeric conspiracies, but responsible men, who know that a culture which does not flourish in action remains an empty culture, the mother of "distinguished failures."

Is it not significant that a second-grade student could write in his school magazine: "The Gangan[3] has more than local value for us; it represents a symbol, the symbol of the many difficulties which confront young nations like ours . . . Gangan . . . We shall only succeed by emulating the Alpine climbers, by holding hands and roping ourselves together."

That is the new climate in which the process of decolonization is unfolding itself.

Stage plays exalting the great moments of African resistance to colonialism are multiplying.

Poems and songs chanting the construction of independence are spreading throughout the country. In all that there is no trace of racial hatred, of revengeful chauvinism, but a determination to discern and apply what corresponds in the first place to national necessities.

Tomorrow, new African nations will regain their sovereignty. The cultural efforts undertaken by Guinea furnish the proof, here and now, that they too, in their reconquered independence, will be able to shatter the ancient forms of alienation and construct the foundations for a "new and solemn departure."

NOTES

1. Article published in "Le Droit de Vivre," October 1956.

2. Extract from the Report on Doctrine and General Policy presented to the Fifth Congress of the Democratic Party of Guinea by the Secretary General of the Party, Sékou Touré (September 14–17, 1959).

3. A mountain in Guinea at the foot of which is situated the Kindia Training College.

A CONTRIBUTION TO THE DEBATE
ON NATIONAL POETRY

Much has been written about poetry. Subtle essayists, distinguished "anatomists" have patiently looked into the mechanism of the poetic act.

Their results have not always measured up to their efforts. The reason is that poetry, although far from being the "profound" mystery in which some initiates want to bury it, defies the rigors of current analysis and the precepts of handbooks.

But since we must give a definition, no matter how vague, of poetry, let us say that it is the harmonious fusion of the sensible with the intelligible, the faculty of achieving through sound and meaning, through image and rhythm, the intimate union of the poet with the world which surrounds him. Poetry, the natural language of life, springs forth and renews itself through its contact with reality. It dies in corsets and under orders.

That is why we do not think that one form, more than another, can give poetry a "national character," or that it suffices to lock up one's inspiration in a so-called traditional mold in order to christen it popular poetry.

The "national" element in such matters is not defined by exterior marks but through psychological peculiarities, through habits of thought produced by given conditions of life, which, through the personal genius of the author, reveal a culture common to people who live in the same nation.

Let us take a precise example. There is no doubt that there was a time in France when the alexandrine was the form most commonly used. Innumerable examples are witnesses to the fact that the alexandrine was admirably suited to the French genius.

But to limit "national character" to the use of fixed forms would mean denying the worth of experiences which, by leading to free verse, have unquestionably contributed new blood to French letters. That would amount to considering the "national" as something immobile, whereas it is a phenomenon susceptible to change simultaneously with the material bases of the nation. We must therefore put in its proper place—a less than secondary one—the question of the superiority of one form over another.

Let the poet draw from the best that is in him whatever reflects the essential values of his country, and his poetry will be national. Better, his poetry will be a message for all, a brotherly message which crosses borders, the important thing being at the start what Césaire calls the right to take the initiative, that is, freedom of choice and action.

Black Africa was systematically deprived of that freedom. Indeed, colonialism seized its material wealth, dislocated its old communities, and swept away its cultural past in the name of a civilization declared "universal" for the occasion. This "vocation for the universal" was not, however, accompanied by the will to transform the Peulh from Fouta, or the Baoulé from the Ivory Coast, into a citizen enjoying the same rights as the good peasant of Beauce or the Parisian intellectual. It was simply a matter of bestowing on a number of Africans an educational veneer necessary and sufficient for having on the spot a herd of auxiliaries ready for all tasks.

Of course, teaching local languages in school was out of the question. So was teaching—even in the imposed tongue—the true history of the great empires of the continent. "Our ancestors the Gauls," etc. It was in such conditions that modern African poets had to resort to the means of expression proper to the colonizers.

The dangers of this are sized up at once: (1) The African creator, deprived of the use of his language and cut off from his people, might turn out to be only the representative of a literary trend (and that not necessarily the least gratuitous) of the conquering nation. His works, having become a perfect illustration of the assimilationist policy through imagination and style, will doubtless rouse the warm applause of a certain group of critics. In fact, these praises will go mostly to colonialism, which, when it can no longer keep its subjects in slavery, transforms them into docile intellectuals patterned after Western literary fashions. Which, besides, is another, more subtle form of bastardization.

(2) Originality at all costs is also a danger. Under the pretext of faithfulness to "Negritude," the African artist could indulge in "inflating" his poems with terms borrowed from the indigenous language, and in systematically searching for a "typical" cast of mind. Hoping "to resurrect the great African myths" through excessive drumbeats and tropical mysteries, he would in fact send back to the colonial bourgeoisie the reassuring image which it wishes to see. That is the surest means of manufacturing "folklore" poetry which will make an impression only in parlors where "negro art" is talked about.

There is hardly a need to stress the fact that the African poet, conscious of his mission, refuses assimilation and facile Africanism at the same time. He knows that by writing in a tongue which is not that of his brothers, he cannot truly translate the "deep song" of his country. But by stressing the presence of Africa with all its contradictions and its faith in the future, by striving through his writings for the end of the colonial regime, the black creator who writes in French contributes to the rebirth of our national cultures.

Who cares, then, whether his ample and hard song bursts forth in alexandrines or in free verse, as long as it pierces the eardrums of those who do not want to hear it, and cracks like whips upon the egoisms and conformisms of order. Form is present only to serve idea, and the only inheritance with any value is the tenderness of a poem by Eluard, the radiant lucidity of Nazim Hikmet, and the "unleashed storm" of Pablo Neruda.

Surely in an Africa freed from oppression it will not occur to any writer to express, otherwise than in his rediscovered language, his feelings and the feelings of his people. And in this sense Francophone African poetry, cut off from its popular roots, is historically doomed.

But by choosing, despite such limitations, to depict the man close to whom he lives, the man whose struggles and sufferings he sees, the African poet will not be forgotten by future generations of our country. He will be read and commented on in our schools and will recall the heroic age when men subjected to the harshest moral and spiritual pressures were able to keep intact their will to progress.

We know that some people wish to see us abandon militant poetry (a term which "purists" jeer at) for the benefit of stylistic exercises and formal discussions. Their hopes will be dashed, since for us, poetry cannot be led to "tame the language beast" but to reflect on the world and to keep the memory of Africa

> Like a splinter in the wound,
> Like a guardian fetish at the center of the village.

Only thus can we fully carry out our responsibilities and prepare the renewal of our civilizations.

AFRICAN POETS

A. R. Bolamba, *Esanzo*. Présence Africaine, 1955.
F. N'dsitouna, *Laterite Flowers* (*Fleurs de latérite*).
K. Paulin Joachim, *A Negro Tells* (*Un Nègre raconte*).
Imprimerie des Poètes, 1954.
Martial Sinda, *First Song of Departure* (*Premier chant du départ*). Seghers, 1955.

"African poets whom I have had a chance to read do not seem to care much about form. This is understandable, of course, since they primarily want to be militant. Entirely absorbed in the struggle they are waging, 'they do not brood,' they do not polish their writings. The urgency of their fight does not agree with the slow and meticulous labor from which a perfect work of art is born."

Such was the answer of a well-known literary critic whose opinion I had sought on Francophone African poetry. It is true that black poets have, in most cases, gone beyond the level of personal experimentation in order to join the great themes of the collective struggle against racism and oppression. Rare are those whose inspiration is not strongly marked by the colonial drama, whether in regretting "the primitive freshness of the black country" or in chanting an Africa bound for progress and freedom. But there are poets for whom those problems do not constitute a prevailing element of their creative activity and who are happy to listen to songs and legends of Africa, to describe its sunny landscape, its dizzying dances. Thus A. R. Bolamba, a Congolese poet. Is it prudence ("We know the peculiar . . . severity of the royal administration") which incites Bolamba to stay away from themes which are too dangerous? For it is impossible for him to have seen of his country only what he is saying. Besides, I have the impression that in his poem "Lokolé," the Congolese poet lets us read his mind.

62

Lokolé
I hear a roar of defeat in the woods
I hear rattlings
Of selfishness
Room for the spirit
Enthroned in my heart
In my heart is the sound of
Victorious trumpets
Victorious Lokolé
My Victory, our victory.

At times the image springs, colored, glowing, pregnant with an all-African sap.

Hills put their backs up
And jump over brooks
Which turn around the calabash
Of the Great Spirit

With Francis N'dsitouna the tone becomes harsh and the emotion changes its quality when we breathe the violent perfume of his *Laterite Flowers*. We at once enter an Africa which is struggling against the monstrous contradictions of a hard world; the Africa of the whip and injustice, which yet does not despair of its future. Perhaps they won't find in N'dsitouna what aestheticians call the breath of "pure poetry" (really, what exactly is "pure poetry"?). He might be reproached with excessive dryness of expression. The fact remains that the author of *Laterite Flowers* personifies today's poet, the one for whom art is nothing without continuation into action.

In his collection *A Negro Tells*, Kokou-Joachim more particularly reveals an African lost and dreaming in a foreign land. His look pierces the European fog in order to pause on an Africa vibrating with rhythms and songs, in order to reassure an anxious mother. Oh, that love, that cult of the mother among Africans! It illuminates all his writings. We must also take notice of Kokou-Joachim's humor, a grating humor, wrapped as it were in a discreet bitterness. For my part I dislike the too idyllic description of a primeval Africa opposed to a technological Europe. But when we measure the violence of our age, may we not dream, at times, of a past which was undoubtedly less selfish and less cruel?

Last, Martial Sinda, about whom we do not wish to believe that only the unjust refusal of a scholarship suddenly "inspired him to a great revolt," makes himself our vigorous spokesman when he writes:

> Face up to the night
> Face up, struggling brothers and friends,
> To the lies of our Masters
> For
> Soon
> The tomtom, gong of human justice
> Will sound with a crash.

There are charming verses, with unequivocal sensuality. Thus:

> You cannot dance
> Ni wala of the hands
> Ni wala of the breasts
> Ni wala of the belly
> Ni wala of the loins
> Ni wala of the Congo, the River-Negress
> With black thighs like a diadem of the rainbow.

For negroes sing also of love, love which ultimately constitutes the supreme goal of their fight. Read these young poets and you will discover in them a single concern: the brotherhood of man. And they do not neglect form all that much. Their form is simply not the form of the "tyrants of language."

COMMENTARY

David Mandessi Diop was born in Bordeaux on July 9, 1927, of a Senegalese father (Diop) and a Cameroonian mother (Mandessi). In Africa more than elsewhere, exogamy is ill regarded. Joyce Cary wove the subplot of a novel around North-South hatreds in Nigeria, and African writers such as Chinua Achebe and Cyprian Ekwensi, in contrast with those Negritudinists who took Europe for their whipping boy, explored indigenous xenophobia in most of their novels, thus preparing the ground for a crop of younger writers who relish smashing African icons. For all that, the "in-laws" of intertribal marriages frequently remain strangers in their new surroundings.

The pan-African Diop-Mandessi family suffered no such difficulties. In Cameroon, Senegal, or France, the children of this marriage showed deep devotion to their parents, who labored long and hard for their health, education, and welfare; and their Cameroonian and Senegalese friends proudly considered them fully authentic Africans. No wonder they all grew up intellectually curious and embarked on careers such as journalism, management, teaching, and medicine.

David's father died in the nineteen-thirties, and he himself had to fight for life almost from birth onward. His survival is due to that miraculous care of which only a mother knows the secret. Madame Diop moved to 32, rue des Ecoles, in Paris, across the street from Présence Africaine's headquarters; and her apartment has remained a shrine for the many friends whom its pleasant personality attracted. Meanwhile, the delicate, intense teen-ager attended the Lycée Marcelin Berthelot, where he studied the sciences and the humanities simultaneously; he voraciously read Césaire, and any other material of Negro interest which he could find in the rich library of his brother-in-law, Alioune Diop. David's schoolboy poems showed promise which drew praises from his elders.

The poet's health took a turn for the worse in 1947, just as he was beginning medical studies at the University of Montpellier. Then there were long stays in hospitals, after which he gave up the medical curriculum for one in liberal arts. He is fondly remembered in Montpellier for his active participation in protest meetings during the Algerian war. On January 21, 1956, rightist thugs chased a demonstrator into David's apartment, roughed up the Africans there, and smashed furniture. No effort was made to bring the culprits to justice.

In 1950 David married Virginie Kamara, later celebrated in his poem "Rama Kam," whose title is an anagram of her name. Virginie's father was a doctor, and she became a nurse. She and David had three children at the time of their divorce in 1958.

Before the publication of *Coups de Pilon* in 1956, five poems by Diop had appeared in Léopold Sédar Senghor's anthology of Negro and Malagasy poetry, and the magazine *Présence Africaine* had published a number of his articles and reviews. His fame soon spread among the numerous nationalist groups in French-speaking Africa, and he became a reigning poet of anticolonialism. When Sékou Touré wrested control of Guinea from the French in 1958, thereby ending the "tutelary era," and de Gaulle retaliated by withdrawing experienced French administrators and teachers from the country, David was among the first Africans to come to the rescue of the revolution. He taught in Kindia, Guinea, for two years, and then accepted the directorship of the Société Africaine de Culture in Dakar. Before assuming this office he decided to submit the manuscript of a second book of poems to his publisher in Paris, take a holiday, and gather documents for his new assignment. He set out from Dakar and never returned. He and his second wife and their two children, with all his papers, vanished in an airplane crash over the Atlantic on August 25, 1960.

ASSESSING DAVID MANDESSI DIOP

When David Diop's first and last volume of poems appeared in 1956, his anger with colonialism had obviously not been exhausted by the earlier satiric poems published in L. S. Senghor's 1948 *Anthologie*. Diop had grown into an adult activist in the meantime, and he promised his inner self to repudiate the condescending remarks by which the older and more famous poet introduced Diop's youthful yet brilliant exercises to the public. These were Senghor's remarks:

> We have no doubt that as he grows older David Diop will
> develop in humanity. He will understand that what makes
> the Negritude of a poem is less its theme than its
> style, the warmth of feeling that gives life to words,
> that transmutes the said into the spoken.

With the dawn of liberal imagination in Africa, even a towering personality like Senghor will have a hard time selling such dogmatic pronouncements. His attempt to straitjacket David Diop was uncalled for. Diop matured in age between 1948 and 1956, but his Negritude remained just as strident. A great poet, with a temperament comparable to Marlowe's or Rimbaud's, Wole Soyinka's or John P. Clark's, David Diop tried to make his theme and style fuse into each other, correct, reinforce, and nourish each other.

AN AFRICAN MARXIST

The Marxist wing of the Negritude movement insisted that writers turn to the problems of the present colonial crisis. They must study the new relation of man to society, Africans to Europeans, and ultimately help create a new society where men of all races and nationalities may feel at home. Their spokesman, Frantz Fanon, declared that the poet must display "a constant concern with specifying the historic moment of the struggle, with limiting

69

the field in which action will unfold, the ideas around which the popular will is to crystallize."

David Diop observed those Marxian formulas more closely and more successfully than any other poet. With each one of his poems he swept away the airy cobwebs of his older and more famous Negritude companions: Senghor, Césaire, Damas, Dadié, Laleau, Rabemananjara, and the others whose concern is less completely based on Marxist materialism.

David Diop's hero is not any one person, nor is his villain. There are only the colonized and the colonizers, the people and its enemy. The villain is not an individual, but the colonial system. The African people, the "wretched of the earth," are the hero and heroine, for they are now a superindividual, reminiscent of the one Jules Romains forged in *Les Hommes de Bonne Volonté*. A common bond has united them into a true community of the oppressed, and the revolutionary spirit that unites them animates each one. That is why Diop uses appeals such as "Listen comrades" and incorporates words like *brothers, brotherly* whenever possible. All for one and one for all is the rule which sustains the common consciousness of a common cause and the common effort for the attainment of liberation and independence.

"Afrique," "Les Vautours," "Rama Kam," and "Le Temps du Martyre," for instance, are never crude in the effort to inculcate Negritude doctrine, despite the fact that they are obviously written by a Marxist poet. Certainly the colonialists are caricatured as inhuman, criminal, vulture-like, and arrogant, but it is done as only a man of genius can do it, with conviction and overwhelming power. In fact, it can be said that these poems are sympathetic to the adversaries. Otherwise, why would Diop, whose gift for last lines is obvious, envision the millennium of universal brotherhood so often, even when the cause of the African revolution is at best uncertain? These last lines, for example, breathe optimism:

This is the song whose only guide is love.
Spring will put on flesh under our steps of light.
The song that carries us to the gardens of life.

Cracking the settled gloom of a thousand years.
The fraternal sign that will come and feed the dream of men.
Will see the gestures of happiness take new form.
And that we together will unfold on the highways of the world.

Diop has the natural touch of an artist who intuitively knows that even his Negritude brand of "socialist realism" must bow to the very essence of art, that is, total freedom of the imagination to follow its own inner sympathies and promptings. When imagination combines with generosity within one and the same poet, as is the case here, it lends a unique life to poetry. And generous David Diop was. He dedicated the first poem and the entire *Coups de Pilon* to his mother. Other poems are marked for those leaders he admires most in the Negritude movement: Césaire, Alioune Diop, Jwyé. He has a poem for Emmett Till, lynched in 1955 for allegedly whistling at a white woman in Money, Mississippi. Other poems are for the victims of French repression in Africa and Indo-China. The workers of the world, "from the mines of Swaziland to the heavy sweat of Europe's factories," are his people too: those for whom the freedom of Western democracy has been only a mirage. Thus, Diop, who began as a proselyte of Negritude, wrote poems which diverge from their original design, and are much more intimately realistic.

There exists a paradoxical difference between the realisms of Diop and Senghor, and that difference emerges most clearly when we compare their poems about women: "Femme Noire" by the latter poet, and "Rama Kam" and "A une Danseuse Noire" by the former. Senghor's work is anesthetized by too much academic training. One is fascinated by the abundance of allusions to French literature, the Bible, world mythology, African history; but somehow the allusions never blend into the rich, sensuous poem which the title indicates. Senghor, who was born in Africa and has lived mostly in Africa, comes through like an amateur scholar cataloging unfelt sentiments, rather than a serious poet recording a private emotion. By contrast, David Diop, who was born in Bordeaux and lived mostly in France, constantly lets his imagination play over and integrate itself into the scene he is describing. Any part of "A une Danseuse Noire" or "Rama Kam" will testify to this. Despite the biographical evidence, Diop sounds more native than Senghor. Although the latter has been involved more significantly in colonial politics, it is Diop who sounds like an activist, with a pen dipped in his own red blood. The cosmic horizons upon which Senghor seems to insist through phrases like "éclair d'un aigle," "attaches célestes," and "soleils prochains," tend to diffuse the reader's interest, while the steady gaze of Diop shows us a woman of flesh and blood, wet and wild.

The last poem in *Coups de Pilon*, "Nègre Clochard," is a microcosm of the African Negritude Socialist revolution as it unfolds in Diop's twenty-two surviving poems. The idea of the new Africa, liberated Africa, is the real hero of this epic tale, which the poet seems to be telling only by installments, and almost aimlessly. A few poems, like those about love and women, try to recreate the ancestral peace in which brave Africans happily lived the uneventful lives of villagers who followed the rhythm of seasons routinely and toned down their little personal dramas. Lust and love, greed and generosity marked this aimless and selfish animal existence and simultaneously laid the ground upon which the new seed was to be sown. These and many more poems evoke the European rape of Africa. It took that exothermic encounter, with its filth and cruelty, to sow the seed of liberty, to get neighbors to gather to discuss the foreign oppressor.

The African revolt marks the painful birth of the idea of a free Africa, an idea which, in Diop's time, "grows again patiently stubbornly / With fruits that take on little by little / The bitter taste of freedom." Each individual African revolutionary might not know more than a tiny bit of its meaning. That is very acceptable because, for the Marxist Diop, the idea of a free Africa comes to full maturity and power only in the aggregate of revolutionary Africans. When he proclaims, in "Nègre Clochard," that

> . . . the Carnival is dead
> I whet the hurricane for future furrows
> For you we will remake Ghana and Timbuktu . . .
> To the sound of mighty pestle blows,

Diop seems to have foreseen the debacles that were to mark the post-independence era when rulers crushed every latent opposition. In 1956 Diop was willing to go that far in order to give full scope to Africa's manifest destiny. Africa will not know peace until all the renegades are wiped out and the continent is deemed safe and ripe for the dawn of the Marxist state. Had Diop known that the new rulers would turn into wanton murderers and corrupt masqueraders in the name of that same African revolution, he would have committed himself to the new freedom which the writers of the sixties were longing for. The most important difference between the Marxist Negritude of Diop and the naturist Negritude of a Hamidou Kane is in the narrower social scope of the latter. Diop's vast epic has room for men and women, children and adults, rich and poor, oppressors and oppressed, and all the confused and broken strata between. Kane's characters are mostly rural. It is never clear in what way the "ambiguous adventure" is deeply felt as an existentially difficult choice.

NARCISSISM AND THE CULT OF ANCESTORS

Wole Soyinka has said many unkind things about Negritude, the black supremacist literary movement which Césaire, Damas, and Senghor founded in Paris in the 1930s in reaction to the waves of racism which were spreading through Europe from Germany. His famous saying, "A tiger does not sing its tigritude," represents a popular version of a deep philosophical conflict. Soyinka is too intelligent to equate Negritude with any fatalistic recurrence which would negate the possibility of change in history; even for Senghor, the poet who presides over the destiny of Senegal, the return to ancestral sources does not mean that the Senegal of today must be ferried back to 1271, no matter how glorious the ancient Empire of Mali was. Yet a dose of sterile ideological rigidity remains at the marrow of Negritude; won't that rigidity handicap the historical process? Won't that rigidity construct a wall, even a moving wall, which can always keep the march of time from leading Africans into the promised land of the modern world? These are the questions Soyinka and other free-thinking Africans are raising.

Negritude writers did excel in conferring a cyclic dimension upon time. The 1956 poems of Diop, which explore the temporality of colonialism, are representative of that particular sensibility. The anguish which Diop expresses grows out of frustration and into an uncompromisingly tragic vision. Critics have haphazardly insisted on the influence of his extended sojourn in France and of his numerous stays in hospital. It is more important, I think, to see that Diop, like the expatriate Joyce, was all the more intensely preoccupied with those health conditions because he felt that colonialism was bleeding Africa and condemning it to an amnesiac existence. The reviews and articles he published in *Présence Africaine* convey inadequately the urgency of those preoccupations. But "Les Vautours," for example, with its trail of images of butchery, goes right to the point:

> The vultures built in the shadow of their claws
> The bloody monument of the tutelary era . . .
> Laughter gasped its last in the metallic hell of roads
> And the monotonous rhythm of Paternosters
> Covered the groans on plantations run for profit
> O sour memory of extorted kisses
> Promises mutilated by machine-gun blasts

What kind of ideas cross the mind of a sick African, hospitalized in Bordeaux, where he reads in newspapers that French colonialism is wiping out practices and styles that once cemented the Wolofs, the Malinkes, the Dualas, and once lent significance to their lives? It must have been very depressing for Diop to remember Ovid's words in *The Metamorphoses*: "Tempus edax rerum"; to convince himself that within the temporal process man cannot find decisive fulfillment and that his own diseased body, as well as the African civilizations which had been falling apart, must follow the implacable laws of cyclical return and undergo decomposition.

When confronted with the mysteries of time, with colonial turmoils and befuddlements, David Diop does not react with the melancholy composure of a Prince Hamlet ("The time is out of joint. O cursed spite, / That ever I was born to set it right!") or a Henry David Thoreau ("As if you could kill time without injuring eternity"). Instead, he follows the fashion set by remote contemporaries such as James Joyce, T. S. Eliot, William B. Yeats, and dons the mask of a suppressed alarm. That, at least, is the man the reader sees behind "Afrique" and "Nègre Clochard." In order to escape from the indecisive nature of history, David Diop, anxious, sought refuge in the dream of

Africa my Africa
Africa of proud warriors in ancestral savannas
Africa of which my grandmother sings
Beside her faraway river
I never knew you

His Africa was an absolute, "unfelt" abstraction. He knew it, said it unequivocally ("Je ne t'ai jamais connue") and meant it. But as a polemicist, he needed that kind of cultural magnificence and glorious militarism; so he invented them. In "Nègre Clochard" he dropped names such as Sundiata, Chaka, Ghana, Timbuktu, not so much for the intrinsic worth of the object they refer to, but rather because they should crystallize into a solid gold Africa which had never existed and will not exist in the foreseeable future. Africa for Diop was a mental picture of a timeless heaven to which he could flee from this dehumanizing world of colonialism and racism.

And that is precisely the attitude Soyinka finds objectionable: Why do Negritude writers deny time and seek a "return to sources" when cyclical time is known to lead its advocates into a blind alley? The contradiction troubled Diop, but did not paralyze him. Because he instinctively knew who the enemies were, he reprieved himself and aimed his bow at obvious targets.

THE MAIN TARGETS

Diop published only twenty-two poems in his lifetime. They all sparkle with hot, beautiful impudences, making his complete works one long diatribe, an uncompromising denunciation of colonialism and of everyone, African or European, who excused or justified its existence in any manner. The reader is fascinated by the ever-renewed examination of the same subject. The sheer quantity of metaphors, similes, aphorisms, sarcasms, and epithets makes up the type of superb scurrility that lies beyond the capacity of an ordinary Negritude poet. Of course, Damas, Césaire, Senghor, Tirolien, Roumain, and many others had established a tradition of satiric Negritude literature with which Diop was familiar. These older writers, especially Césaire, had a vivacity and picturesqueness of vituperation that must have pleased Diop greatly. Though the latter took some technical and thematic hints from the aging pioneers, he managed to keep his distance from them: often to match their talent, and always to surpass them in hortatory eloquence and in intensity of passion.

In the course of his twenty-two poems, David Mandessi Diop rises against the cruelty of man to man, all forms of oppression, wars, humiliating arrogance, greed and exploitation, insensitivity and thoughtlessness, the hypocrisy and idiocy of pride in civilization. The *pieds-noirs*, who embody colonialism, emerge from his fiery poems as killers, rapists, torturers, and much worse, but such epithets do not reveal the creative talent behind the details, and the major aspects of the composition, of those poems.

The title of the first poem in *Coups de Pilon*, "A ma Mère," is subtle, skilfully chosen, and eloquent. It points not just to his Cameroonian mother ("O mother mine") who, as a young widow, cared for him during his long stays in hospitals. It also points to the more general Mother Africa, "mother of all," who wields a unifying and magnetic power over the consciences of all black men, who has been cruelly raked over by despots, slave traders, colonialists and contemporary tyrants, and who, above all, symbolizes the hope for a cyclical return to happiness, the hope for the rebirth and rejuvenation of the race.

The first seven lines of that poem suggest with dramatic force the futile arrogance and the ever-present physical perils that haunt life in a colony. The self-indulgent aristocrats have triumphed and their indecent joys can only nauseate the proud, though vanquished, Africans. This grimly realistic picture of colonialism is followed by a celebration of motherhood: lips, smiles, patience. The contrast between colonialism and the dual mother (genetrix and Motherland) is very effectively sustained.

"O mother mine" is not an evocation of happiness, for the spectacle of life, mingling colonialism with motherhood, did not quiet the conscience of the poet. He has dreadful visions of black slaves breaking the chains that hold them in bondage. The struggle goes on and hope will not die. There is cause for indignation and grim determination, but not for despair, for, dialectically, the world has not retrogressed, and the forces of love are armed with conviction and passionate intensity:

> Listen listen to the voice
> This is the cry shot through with violence
> This is the song whose only guide is love.

Léopold Senghor voiced similar hopes in "Le Kaya-Manga" and "Prière aux masques" among others, but his calling Africans "hommes de la danse" is romantic, insincere and indicative of the nature of "formulism," that trend of thought which has, more than anything else, sown clichés about Africa and Africans in the four corners of the earth. Senghor's formulas lack that implacable truthfulness which marks the popular aspirations of Siegfried Sassoon and Wilfred Owen, Bertolt Brecht and Yevgeny Yevtushenko, or, closer to our topic, Yambo Ouologuem and David Mandessi Diop. The pain of colonial existence is recreated in Diop, while there is, in Senghor's writing, a certain dilettantism which suggests that his Negritude is more a self-sufficient intellectual exercise than a real, heartbreaking commitment.

"A ma Mère," the seminal poem in *Coups de Pilon*, shares with Diop's other poems an unmistakable epic magnificence and a clearly audible quality, both of which make the Senegalo-Cameroonian poet a favorite for public readings. The present writer recalls readings before audiences in various corners of the North American continent, and was most impressed by the visceral response forthcoming in the Washington State Reformatory at Monroe near Seattle, Washington. He was constantly interrupted by exclamations such as "Right on!" "Yea!" "Tell 'em!", and by many other much less reproducible groans of total approval. Those prisoners, who were all black, perceived and visualized a condition which David Diop had expressed, a contradiction between the heroic ancestral past and the ignominious colonial present. Diop, who always managed to transcend the here and now for the benefit of the universal and the eternal, projected the resolution of that contradiction into a future age of freedom for all. No wonder prisoners, who lived on hope, cheered so loudly.

They cheered "Afrique," for example, which evokes the martial glories of pre-colonial Africa and the pride with which soldiers served Sundiata and Chaka. In contrast with those proud warriors and the dithyrambic songs they inspired, European conquerors were pitiful indeed, since all they did was shed blood, enslave children, and emasculate adults. But Diop, that "fils impétueux," belongs to the emerging generation, one that came of age simultaneously with the Bandoeng Conference and the Mau-Mau revolt. Since older Negritude poets could not restore liberty and justice, Diop offered to assume that task himself.

> Impetuous son the young and hardy tree
> You see there
> Splendidly alone among white and faded flowers
> Is Africa your Africa . . .

Observers of the African scene are familiar with a certain puerile vanity that puffs up political speeches. But there is a difference in this poem. First, the speaker is not a brainless politician inflating the worth of his own schemes, but an archetypal, "grave" ancestor voicing his hope for the future of his impetuous son. Secondly, that ancestor is assigning the task of a David (intended equivocation and ambiguity on the part of the author?) to his son, who must fight the colonial Goliath. The biblical coloring which Diop lends to that speech gives the poem a dignity and majesty comparable to the greatest visions of revolutionary poetry: the poet has progressed in depth and breadth by moving from political diatribe to prophetic invective.

The best poem Diop ever wrote is probably "Nègre Clochard," the last in *Coups de Pilon*, dedicated to the writer Diop admired most, Aimé Césaire. More precisely, the Aimé Césaire of *Cahier d'un Retour au Pays Natal* and *Discours sur le Colonaialisme*, rather than the Gaullist of later times. "Nègre Clochard" blends epic and satiric themes. The hero is famous because he has fought hopeless battles against a hostile world, whereas the narrator has used up his life in a marathon carnival. In an artistic *tour de force*, Diop organically unifies the poem by making the speaker promise to abandon his happy-go-lucky ways in order not only to avenge the "Negro tramp" but also to rebuild Africa.

The poem is divided into three parts. The first twenty-eight lines are devoted to the odyssey of the hero, an odyssey that reads like a string of failures: "old broken dream," "accepted pain," "negro blood," "thorns of your tattered clothes," "crouching stops of despair," "bellies opening," "naked in your filthy jail," "extinct volcano," "Snow White." By this catalog the poet shows how much ridicule has covered Africans throughout recent history.

And failure is precisely what makes this an epic poem in the best tradition of the genre. The illogical condemnation of Meursault to death, together with the destruction of any hope for a life without illusion here on earth, gives Camus's *L'Etranger* a grandeur that no acquittal could match. In *La Chanson de Roland*, Roland and Olivier are more victorious in their failure and subsequent death than they could ever dream of being under different circumstances. In Diop's poem too, the "Negro tramp" is triumphant in defeat. Physical and psychological suffering heightens the effect by arousing sympathy which good fortune would leave inoperative.

The next thirteen lines describe the drifting life of the speaker, the prototype of the "bon nègre" or, even more concretely, the dancing Africans of Timbuktu and Saõ Tomé whom Lope de Vega celebrated in his *Canto de los Negros*. Diop's language is always vigorous, precise, and endowed with a great sweep:

> What did I do but bear seated on my clouds
> Nocturnal agonies

Immovable wounds
Petrified rags . . .
And I saw that day just like other days
And I sang Yeba
Yeba in utter madness zoos in delirium
O buried plants
O lost seeds

This excerpt reveals Diop at his poetic best, since it expresses with a great deal of power the fundamental thought from which all the other variations and elaborations spring: anxiety about a colonialism which ruins the mind, degrades the personality, misleads or exasperates lucid believers, and allows only hardy souls to persist in thoughtful action and devotion to the good of their fellows.

The dehumanizing process inherent in colonialism is admirably suggested. Diop skilfully depicts the implacable consequences of passivity and inaction: "But I I what did I do?" The question is rhetorical, since the narrator will go on to tell us what he did and implicitly what he failed to do. It is also effectively repeated a few lines later to make the reader feel, with the speaker, that there is sincere regret for not having waged an honorable war against the European Conquistadors and for the liberation of Africans. Will the curse of colonialism last forever?

The answer in the third and last part of the poem is a resounding No. Here, Diop, aware of the anticolonialist works of Mao Tse-tung and Ho Chi Minh, Ruben Um Nyobe and Felix Moumié, Jomo Kenyatta and Kwame Nkrumah, evokes the Black Revolution or, more largely, the revolution of "les damnés de la terre" (some six years before Frantz Fanon!), taken at the height of the conflict. It is a picture ablaze with colorful exploits, contrasting with the preceding one which is shrouded in passivity. In the flames of battle, the revolutionaries "whet the hurricane" despite, or perhaps because of, the obvious danger that in the process of rebuilding Ghana and Timbuktu with such a cosmic exhuberance, the whole earth may founder.

Poems of a different mold mingle with these compositions of epic stature. They deal with nature. Colonialism for Diop is opposed to nature and to liberty. Since liberty is a natural state, one may hope it will prevail. In some of these poems, external nature not only contributes a great deal to the beauty and originality of the whole, but also contrasts beautifully with vile colonialism. That at least is what we find in "Certitude":

> To those who grow fat on murders
> And measure the stages of their reign in corpses
> I say that days and men
> Sun and stars
> Shape the fraternal rhythm of the peoples.

Even the potential benefits of European technology and other forms of mastery over nature are wasted in thoughtlessness, as we see in "A un Enfant Noir":

> In air-conditioned mansions
> Around cool drinks
> An easy conscience relishes its rest.

Ultimately the poet seeks to make nature identical with hope for the future, and symbolic of the liberty of oppressed people everywhere. Hence colonialism can fight nature ($=$ liberty) for awhile, but nature will always win the final victory:

> Do you hear the sap rumble underground
> It is the song of the dead
> The song that carries us to the gardens of life.

> All who were drugged with fatality
> Launch their immense song amid the waves
> The raging waves of freedom
> That slap slap against the maddened Beast.

External nature also plays a more conventional role in these and numerous other instances, by simply supplying the background, often the luxuriantly green background of tropical forests, in which Diop places masters and slaves or a narrative. In "A un Enfant Noir," a typical American landscape (skyscraper, air-conditioner, Bible-waving fundamentalists, parties, jazz, etc.) surrounds the whites who lynched Emmett Till. The narrative of that tragedy, insignificant on the canvas of contemporary history, incites the poet to evoke a greater tragedy, the dullness of the conscience of the whites.

Another important aspect of Diop's cult of nature is love. He included three love poems in *Coups de Pilon*, and we can understand them better by comparing them with Senghor's "Femme Noire," for there are in contention here two different kinds of love. A "Femme Noire" was the person to conjure with when the Negritudinists strung their lutes to the theme of love. She represented, with a difference, the Platonic conception of love for all the black race. That difference resided in the physical proximity of the partners and in the down-to-earth sensuality of the female. Senghor's poem reflects none of these characteristics, and the reader wants to dispose of it by throwing at the poet the lines Lord Byron wrote in *Don Juan*:

> Think you if Laura had been Petrarch's wife
> He would have written sonnets all his life?

Senghor's ideal and intangible black woman is set, like an idol, on a pedestal. The poet provides us with no details of her physical appearance or about her character. Nakedness and blackness by themselves start streams of disjointed dreams and emotions, suggestions and images, all of which, more than the black woman herself, constitute the vortex of the poem. The title alone, "Femme Noire," deprived as it is of any defining article, prepares the mind for a space odyssey, in the course of which we are likely to encounter only pure, graceful, black angels.

Diop, however, evokes sensuous beauty and physical passion, the magnetic force that draws man to woman instinctively, irresistibly. Rama Kam, for instance, in the poem of that name which sings the poet's love for his first wife, is associated with images of wild animals, ripe fruits, hot spices, tropical heat and languor, unadulterated sensuality, and earth-shaking forces of nature. This is physical pleasure at its rawest, evoking the violent rise of passion at the beginning, the erotic sensations, the sound and fury of fireworks, and concluding with the breathless tenderness that follows orgasm. This, also, by its relentless adhesion to concrete and particular reality, is more poetry than anything Senghor ever wrote.

One aspect of Diop's poetry which is often overlooked is his humor. Gerald Moore, in *Seven African Writers*, wants to see him always singing an African "Marseillaise," always serious and oracular. Granted that David Diop exhibits the tragic and austere appearance of a giant compelled to support the heavens on his shoulders; yet we should imagine him happy and satisfied at the sudden termination of a convulsive journey. His polemic talent provides the reader with revolutionary humor, laughter complicated by animosity, mocking laughter as well as vengeful laughter, irony as well as indignation.

Aiming at the *literati*, Diop attacks those Africans whom academic honors have intoxicated. He has not forgotten the patronizing comments of an *agrégé de grammaire*, L. S. Senghor, in his 1948 anthology. Not only does Diop dedicate no poem to Senghor (other big names were so honored: Alioune Diop, Aimé Césaire) but also he veils rather thinly some of his allusions in, for instance, "A une Danseuse Noire":

> And around me the myths burn
> Around me burn the wigs of learning
> In great fires of joy in the sky of your steps . . .
> The false gods burn beneath your vertical flame . . .
> You are the idea of the All and the voice of the Ancient.
> Gravely launched to attack chimeras
> You are the Word . . .

Academia ("the wigs of learning") as well as Christianity ("the Word") and indigenous religions ("false gods," "chimeras"), all are put to shame before the existential merits of an incendiary black beauty.

Diop might well have suspected that intellectuals would continue to tease their own pedantic brains even after independence. That his vision remains correct is all too easy to prove. A Pickwickian black professor, graduate of a famous French university, begins each school year with a "cours inaugural," to which he invites, among others, the semi-literate establishment. His speech is a string of polysyllables (*tératologie, grammatologie* are among his favorites), which are carefully distributed throughout the lecture for greatest effect. Whenever things get too obscure, the audience takes it as a sign of depth and applauds. Whenever his more perceptive colleagues express displeasure about the show, Black Pickwick replies: "As long as education is not possible in Africa, an intellectual who wants to prosper must devote himself to miseducation." Such things are happening in Africa many years after independence and David Diop's death.

But it is colonialism, with its European and African servants, that provides Diop with his best themes of furious laughter. In the nineteen-fifties Africa was filled with handpicked spokesmen whom the French used in order to thwart nationalistic aspirations and to perpetuate their dominion. Diop, responsive to a subject which South Africa's James Matthews will exploit more fully and more wittily in his short story, "Azikwelwa," imagines these politicians in his "Le Renégat," making the rounds of cocktail parties in Paris:

> My brother with teeth that flash to hypocritical compliments
> My brother with gold-rimmed glasses
> Over eyes turned blue by the Master's word
> My poor brother with silk-lined dinner jacket
> Squeaking and droning and strutting in the parlors of condescension
> We find you pitiable . . .

Against whites in colonies, he uses some of the most biting ironies conceived since Jonathan Swift. "Le Temps du Martyre," "Un Blanc m'a dit," and "Souffre, pauvre Nègre," all published in 1948 and exposing the teleological proposition that Africans are meant to be slaves, are doubtless among the most savagely sustained ironic poems of our time. The first, from the biblical allusion "Martyre" in the title to the very last verse, deals with colonial man's moral nature and the defective systems that he creates out of his own imperfections. It is distinguished by clear and concrete diction, simple syntax, economy of words, controlled style, fiery indigation:

> The White killed my father
> My father was proud
> The White raped my mother
> My mother was beautiful
> The White beat my brother under the sun of the roads
> My brother was strong
> The White turned toward me
> His hands red with black blood
> And said in his Master's voice:
> "Boy! An easy chair, a towel, water!"

This ferocious indictment of Europe, and beyond it, of all oppressors, has become a favorite battle hymn of pan-Negrism. It gives pleasure to blacks in Harlem and Sophiatown, in Kingston and Duala. Diop's imagination could not have received a better tribute. "Un Blanc m'a dit" also shows his obsession with man's inhumanity to man, especially when man hides savagery behind a civilized façade and takes inordinate pride in himself. The effect of European follies on Africans is the theme of "Souffre, pauvre Nègre." Only a satirical genius could realize that you had only to weld masters and slaves to their respective roles to make both look contemptible, ridiculous, and disgusting. The horror of the poem lies not only in the whites' degeneration but also and mainly in the poor Negro's realization that he too can undergo moral regression by simply accepting the image of himself he receives from his masters.

CONCLUDING REMARKS

I have tried to explain *Coups de Pilon* through a systematic analysis of the poems, through relating those poems to the author's biography, culture, and psychology, and through consideration of his intentions and of their conceptual significance. I have insisted throughout on the formal interest and the fundamental intelligence of Diop's slim volume. Now let me treat it as a vehicle of Third World culture.

This son of Senegal and Cameroon looks like a paragon of the cosmopolitan bourgeoisie, provided with leisure, money, famous and mundane literary acquaintances. Like Gide or Proust, Diop writes in fragments and at leisure, at least in the beginning. But soon the bourgeois clichés break down, and the pleasurable accumulation of culture begins to destroy this Diop and transform him into the author of bigger works. Fate did not allow him to leave behind the manuscripts that would have lent even more density and breadth to an already very cosmopolitan production.

Between 1958 and 1960, weakened by poor health and excited about political developments in Francophone Africa, David Diop finds himself involved on many fronts of the struggle for liberation from the colonial yoke. A major interest of *Coups de Pilon* resides in its success in revealing the writer's individuality during this crucial period: a "creative emotion" permeates the poems and serves as the backdrop on which the author prints the singularity of his genius. Every piece in the volume is, to paraphrase Keats, a meeting-place for the soul poet and his soul reader. This is the literary miracle which comes about only through a radiance of beauty, through its correspondence with the intensity of a consciousness.

As a Negritudinist Diop had to meet new demands, based on the knowledge that the individual is no longer sufficient. Even transcendent genius has become only a step toward a total truth of love and knowledge, the truth of Negritude, the beginning and end of any black genius. Such mysticism, although understandable in its context, has become a bore for most readers, black and others. Mystic Negritude can make sense with regard to some characteristically black situations, such as lynchings and Dimbokro. Diop writes movingly about both because he shares the suffering and believes in the cause. But Diop's Negritude does not abolish dialogue and sympathy, which are his great human qualities. Vietnam and the South interest him because their fighters blend imaginative dynamism with psychological curiosity and fundamental metaphysical intuitions. Using all the "damnés de la terre" as characters in *Coups de Pilon* presents an important advantage: it brings to light the identical reactions of human beings in the face of an enormous and complex drama, a drama sustained by violence and brotherhood, revolt and despair, dream and utopia. The universality of man's inhumanity to man makes the task of a freedom-fighting poet confusing, but Diop's sensitivity succeeds in lending an idea of order to the struggle.

Blow after blow is administered at all aspects of colonialism, and ten years after Diop's death his holy wrath continues to make one recoil. But a pledge accompanied the satiric deluge. I have already pointed out its ramifications in "Nègre Clochard":

> For you we will remake Ghana and Timbuktu . . .
> To the sound of mighty pestle blows

But the original pledge was a categorical assertion of Black Power in 1948, in "Défi à la Force":

> Toi que plies toi qui pleures
> Toi qui meurs un jour comme ça sans savoir pourquoi
> Toi qui luttes qui veilles pour le repos de l'Autre
> Toi qui ne regardes plus avec le rire dans les yeux
> Toi mon frère au visage de peur et d'angoisse
> Relève-toi et crie: NON!

These admirable lines are not idle words. Ancestral Africans, colonial Africans, and independent Africans have one common enemy: oppression. Yambo Ouologuem proved it convincingly in *Devoir de Violence,* as did Ayi Kwei Armah in *The Beautyful Ones Are Not Yet Born.* In "Défi à la Force," a free man, an untrammeled conscience, takes his stand against that same oppression, refuses to yield, and endures the trials of the revolutionary life until his untimely death. In our day of repressive, self-indulgent, lifelong presidencies, we cannot afford to ignore the freedom-generating legacy of David Mandessi Diop.

GLOSSARY

The Ancient. Dead ancestors are objects of many cults because of the powers they retain over the living and because they continue to preserve the communal wisdom.

Aimé Césaire. Born in Martinique in 1913. Called "grand poète noir" by André Breton in 1943 for his surrealistic long poem, *Cahier d'un Retour au Pays Natal*. Coined the term *Négritude,* and has been associated with the pan-Negro cultural renaissance since the nineteen-thirties.

Chaka. A Zulu chieftain of the ninteenth century. One of the most heroic figures in African history. He led his warriors barefoot over thorns to toughen their feet, initiated the use of the stabbing spear to replace the javelin, and relied on the irreversible verdict of hand-to-hand combat. He plunged into sex orgies with the same warlike earnestness.

Dimbokro. A village in the Ivory Coast, scene in 1948 of intense nationalist activity by the Rassemblement Démocratique Africain and harsh repressive measures by the colonial government.

Guardian tree. During initiation rites African boys and girls are taken to this tree for circumcision and clitoridectomy, after which they are regarded as adults.

Kora. An African type of harp. It may have as many as thirty-two strings and is much used in West Africa for accompanying songs and dances.

Mamba. A common name in the Guinea-Ivory Coast border regions.

Poulo Condor. Former name of Con Dao, a group of islands off southern Vietnam. The French used them as penitentiaries for nationalist leaders.

Sundiata. Thirteenth-century king, founder of the empire of Mali.

Word. Nommo, or Word, enables man to establish dominion over things. This belief is widely held in Africa.